Contents

Credits

EDITOR: Wendy Slotboom
COPY EDITOR: Laurie Shifrin
ILLUSTRATIONS AND BOOK DESIGN:
Wendy Slotboom and
Marsha McCloskey
COVER DESIGN: Jason Yenter
PHOTOGRAPHY: Ken Wagner
PHOTO STYLING: Sharon Yenter

More Fat 8ths and Friends
©2006 Marsha McCloskey
In The Beginning, Seattle, Washington USA

ISBN: 0-9706900-8-8
Printed in USA

Introduction

Quilters make quilts for different reasons: for gifts, for home and holiday decor, for charity, for therapy, for competition, for art, and for fun. Making quilts and collecting fabrics adds color, texture, pattern, and sociability to our lives. I collect different types of fabric for different types of quilts. For Feathered Stars, I look for traditional prints with high contrast. For Blended quilts, I look for romantic, large-scale floral prints with lots of colors, but relatively little contrast. When I'm feeling artistic, I like batiks. When I just want to make a fun quilt, the bright, cheerful reproduction prints of the 1930s and 40s, like those found in the *Fat 8ths and Friends* fabric collections, are especially appealing.

In this book you'll find six new quilt patterns. Most are based on traditional block designs like Birds in the Air and Log Cabin, but the Tulips in Bloom quilt is an original design, made just for the *More Fat 8ths and Friends* fabric collection. For a homey, easy-to-piece project, try the Log Cabin blocks in the Apple Orchard quilt on page 6. If you like simple appliqué, check out the Bumbleberry Baskets quilt on page 9. Spring Fancy, on page 21, has a few triangles, but is mostly squares and rectangles. If you don't mind triangles, try Peaches and Cream on page 14, or Out to Sea on page 24. If you want to spend a little more time on your project, then Tulips in Bloom, on page 28, is a great choice.

Whether you quilt by yourself or with friends, and for whatever reasons you make these quilts, I hope you have fun with the patterns, the colors, and the prints.

Marsha McCloskey

Getting Started

All About Fat 8ths

More Fat 8ths and Friends is a collection of six quilt patterns made with reproduction prints from the 1930s and 1940s. These scrappy quilt patterns use a variety of prints and are written for Fat 8ths, or pieces of fabric that measure $10^1/2$" x 18".

Quilt stores often sell precut fat quarter yards, measuring 18" x 21", either one at a time or in coordinated packets. Quilters like them because they provide more useable fabric than quarter yards measured off the bolt at 9". Likewise, a Fat 8th yard allows more useable fabric than a $4^1/2$" strip cut from the bolt. Most quilt stores will not even cut eighths because of the awkward shape of the pieces. Fat 8ths are sometimes offered in 9" x 21" pieces, but we've found those pieces to be less useful than the $10^1/2$" x 18" cuts. By simply cutting fat quarters in half the short way, quilt shops can offer Fat 8ths and provide quilters with a nice selection of prints in this smaller format.

In The Beginning Fabrics is now printing four prints on the same bolt with each print running in a lengthwise stripe (parallel to the selvage) that measures $10^1/2$" wide. Cut a half yard (18") from the bolt, then cut the prints apart and you have four coordinated Fat 8ths! It's a great way to get a wide variety of prints for your collection for not a lot of money.

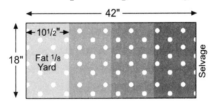

If your fabric is not printed with 4 different prints, you can still cut Fat 8ths. Cut a half yard of fabric (18" x 42"); then divide the half yard in half to make 2 "fat" quarter yards, each measuring

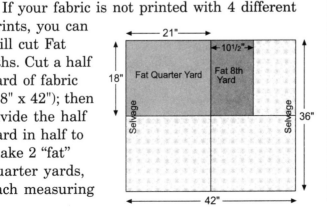

18" x 21". Then divide both fat quarters in half the short way to make a total of 4 Fat 8ths, each measuring $10^1/2$" x 18".

The "Friends" in the book title refers to the additional yardage that is inevitably needed to make a quilt. In the *More Fat 8ths and Friends* fabric collection, there are several coordinating fabrics that are printed just one design on the bolt. These larger pieces are intended for borders, setting pieces, backings, and bindings.

Fat 8th Yields

To prepare my fabric, I rinse it in warm water and dry it in the dryer. I do this before cutting for three reasons: to check for color fastness, to preshrink, and to "rough-up" the surface so that patches don't slip during piecing.

To allow for cutting variations and shrinkage, Fat 8th yields are based on a useable 10" x 17" piece of fabric (ideally $10^1/2$" x 18"). After rinsing, drying, and pressing your Fat 8ths, measure the pieces. If there is not a useable 10" x 17", you may need to buy more fabric. If your piece of fabric is more generous, you may be able to cut more patches than are shown in the diagrams.

Quiltmaking Basics:

Cutting and Piecing

Rotary Cutting

The basic tools for cutting fabric patches are a rotary cutter, ruler, and mat. If you don't already own rotary cutting tools, choose a cutter that fits comfortably in your hand, a self-healing mat, and an acrylic ruler that measures at least 6" x 24" and is marked with measurements in $1/4$" and $1/8$" increments.

If you are new to rotary cutting, practice on scrap fabric first. The blade is very sharp; it is not necessary to press very hard when you first begin, but be sure to place even pressure on the blade as you cut. Always remember to: keep your fingers and other body parts away from the blade, close the blade each time you finish cutting, and keep the cutter out of the reach of children. The cutter can be dangerous if not used with proper care.

Cutting Strips from Yardage

Fold the fabric selvage to selvage, aligning the widthwise and lengthwise grains as best you can. Place fabric on the rotary cutting mat with the folded edge closest to you. Align a square plastic cutting ruler with the fold of the fabric and place a long cutting ruler to the left.

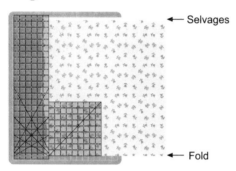

When making all cuts, fabric should be placed to your right. (If you are left handed, reverse the directions.) Remove the square ruler and make a rotary cut along the right side of the long ruler to trim away the uneven raw edges of fabric. Be sure to hold the ruler firmly in place, and roll the cutter away from you, cutting through all layers.

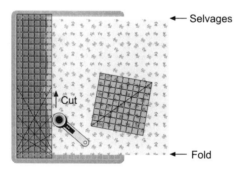

Make successive cuts measuring from the first cut as shown. All strips are cut with the $1/4$" seam allowance included.

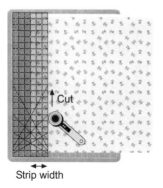

To cut border strips on the lengthwise grain, position the fabric so cuts will be parallel to the selvage. Make the first cut to trim away the selvage and to create a clean edge from which to measure. Make successive cuts measuring from the first cut.

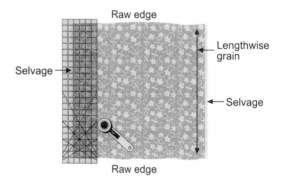

Squares and Rectangles

Measurements given for cutting squares and rectangles include $1/4$" seam allowances. First cut fabric into strips in the width given in the instructions. For squares, using the square plastic cutting ruler, align the top and bottom edge of strip and cut fabric into squares the same width as the strip.

Cut rectangles in the same manner, first cutting strips the width of the rectangle, then cutting to the proper length.

Triangles

Cut fabric in strips, then into squares the size specified in the instructions. The measurements given for half- and quarter-square triangles in the quilt directions include $1/4$" seam allowances.

Half-Square Triangles

If you need a triangle with the straight grain on the short side, cut half-square triangles. Cut a square, then cut it in half diagonally once. The resulting two triangles will have short sides on the straight grain of the fabric and the long side on the bias.

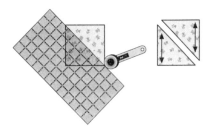

Quarter-Square Triangles

If you need a triangle with the straight grain on the long side, cut quarter-square triangles. Cut a square, then cut it in half diagonally twice. The resulting four triangles will have the long side on the straight grain and the short sides on the bias.

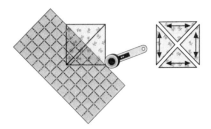

Trimming Triangle Points

Templates are provided for all the triangles in the quilt designs. Use them to trace templates for hand piecing or to check rotary-cut shapes for accuracy. Trimlines shown on triangular templates make it easy to match shapes for sewing. Use the Precision Trimmer 3 as shown to trim triangles where indicated in the quilt patterns and on the templates.

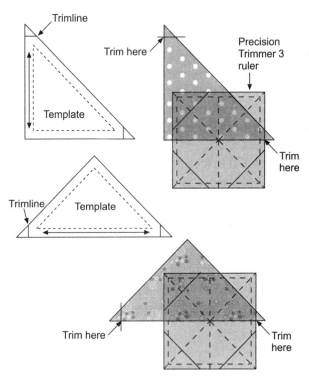

Machine Piecing

To make a pieced block, sew the smallest pieces together first to form units. Join smaller units together, forming larger ones, until the block is complete. Diagrams with each quilt pattern show the order in which to sew the patches together.

Use 100 percent cotton thread as light as the lightest fabric in the project. Sew exact $1/4$" seams. On some machines the width of the presser foot is $1/4$" and can be used as guide. If you don't have such a foot, you'll need to establish the proper seam allowance on your sewing machine. Place a piece of quarter- or eighth-inch graph paper under the presser foot and gently lower the needle onto the line that is $1/4$" from the edge of the paper. Lay a piece of masking tape at the edge of the paper to act as the $1/4$" guide.

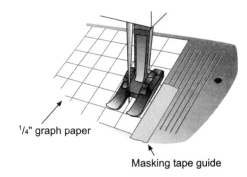

For the patterns in this book, sew from cut edge to cut edge. Backtack if you wish, but when a seam line will be crossed and held by another, it is not necessary. Use chain piecing whenever possible to save time and thread. To chain piece, sew one seam, but do not lift the presser foot. Do not take the piece out of the sewing machine and do not cut the thread. Instead, set up the next seam to be sewn and stitch as you did the first. There will be a little twist of thread between the two pieces. Sew all the seams you can at one time in this way, then remove the "chain." Clip the threads.

Masking tape guide

Pinning

Pin seams before stitching if matching is involved, if your seams are longer than 4", or if your fabrics are a little slippery. Pin points of matching (where seam lines or points meet) first. Once these important points are firmly in place, pin the rest of the seam, easing if necessary.

Pressing

In this book, most seams are pressed to one side, toward the darker fabric whenever possible. Sometimes, for matching purposes, seams are pressed in opposite directions, regardless of which is the darker fabric. Other times seams are pressed open to distribute bulk.

Press with a dry iron that has a shot of steam when needed. Take care not to overpress. First, press the sewn seam flat to "set" it. Next, press the seam open or to the side as instructed. Press from both the right and wrong sides to make the seam flat without little pleats at the ends.

About the Patterns

The six quilt patterns in *More Fat 8ths and Friends* were designed to be easy and fun to make. With the exception of the appliquéd baskets in Bumbleberry Baskets, all the directions are written for rotary cutting and machine piecing. Templates are provided where space permits. When cutting triangles, follow the rotary cutting instructions and compare the cut shapes to the printed templates to check for accuracy.

In the Materials lists, fabric requirements are given in Fat 8ths for the scrappy parts of the quilts and in normal 40"-wide yardage for most setting pieces, borders, bindings, and backings. (The 40"-wide measurement is "useable width." With selvages included, your fabric will be wider.) A fabric requirement that reads, "12 Fat 8ths of assorted prints for blocks" means that you need to buy at least 12 different Fat 8ths to make the block designs. If you find more fabrics than 12, by all means, use them as well. Study the color photographs of the quilts found on the inside front and back covers and in the Quilt Gallery, in the center of the book, to get an idea of the variety of prints needed.

Each pattern includes cutting diagrams to help you get the most out of every Fat 8th. First, read the information on the number of pieces to cut, then look at the Fat 8th cutting diagrams to see how to cut the necessary patches. All cutting instructions include a $1/4$" seam allowance.

Block Dimensions

Measure your sewn blocks for accuracy. When you have made a block for a quilt, it will have a "finished" dimension and an "edge-to-edge" dimension. The "finished" dimension is the measurement of the square without seam allowances, after it is sewn into the quilt. The "edge-to-edge" or raw measurement includes seam allowances and should be $1/2$" larger than the finished dimension. Finished block dimensions are given at the beginning of each pattern. You'll find edge-to-edge dimensions in the piecing instructions.

See quilt finishing instructions on pages 34-36.

Apple Orchard

This Log Cabin variation is so easy, it doesn't even require that you separate the lights and darks. Just pick up a different print rectangle each time you stitch... and try not to place strips of the same prints next to each other.

DESIGNED BY: Marsha McCloskey

QUILTED BY: Carrie Peterson

FINISHED QUILT SIZE: 73" x 84$\frac{1}{2}$"

FINISHED BLOCK SIZE: 11$\frac{1}{2}$" x 11$\frac{1}{2}$"

See this quilt in color on the inside front cover.

Materials

Fabric requirements are based on Fat 8ths (useable measurement: 10" x 17"), or 40" fabric width.

- 36 Fat 8ths of assorted colored prints for blocks
- $\frac{3}{8}$ yd. red tonal print for block centers
- $\frac{5}{8}$ yd. red check for inner border
- 2$\frac{1}{4}$ yds. floral bouquet print for outer border
- $\frac{7}{8}$ yd. green tonal for binding
- 5$\frac{1}{2}$ yds. for backing (lengthwise seam) OR 4$\frac{3}{4}$ yds. (widthwise seam)
- 81" x 93" batting

Directions

See *Quiltmaking Basics,* beginning on page 2, for general cutting and piecing directions. All cutting measurements include $\frac{1}{4}$"-wide seam allowance. Press seams in direction of arrows unless otherwise instructed.

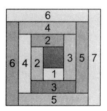

CUTTING

When a number is followed by a second number in parentheses, the first number indicates the pieces needed to make one block. The number in parentheses indicates the pieces needed to make all 30 blocks.

Study Fat 8th cutting diagrams below and then, from Fat 8th assortment of 36 colored prints, first cut lengthwise strips 2" wide, then cut:

- 1 (30) #1 rectangles, 2" x 3", for blocks
- 2 (60) #2 rectangles, 2" x $4\frac{1}{2}$", for blocks
- 2 (60) #3 rectangles, 2" x 6", for blocks
- 2 (60) #4 rectangles, 2" x $7\frac{1}{2}$", for blocks
- 2 (60) #5 rectangles, 2" x 9", for blocks
- 2 (60) #6 rectangles, 2" x $10\frac{1}{2}$", for blocks
- 1 (30) #7 rectangles, 2" x 12", for blocks

#5 (9")		#2 ($4\frac{1}{2}$")	#1 (3")
#5 (9")		#4 ($7\frac{1}{2}$")	
#6 ($10\frac{1}{2}$")		#3 (6")	
#6 ($10\frac{1}{2}$")		#3 (6")	
#7 (12")		#2 ($4\frac{1}{2}$")	

From each of 30 Fat 8ths, cut five 2" x 17" strips. Subcut the strips as shown above.

#4 ($7\frac{1}{2}$")	#4 ($7\frac{1}{2}$")
#4 ($7\frac{1}{2}$")	#4 ($7\frac{1}{2}$")
#4 ($7\frac{1}{2}$")	

You will still need 30 more #4 rectangles. Cut these from the remaining 6 Fat 8ths as shown above. You can also cut extra pieces from these Fat 8ths to mix in your blocks as you sew. You don't want all the blocks to be identical, or to have identical fabrics end up next to each other where the blocks meet.

From red tonal print, cut:
- 1 (30) squares, 3" x 3", for block centers

From red check print, cut:
- 7 strips, 2" x 40", for inner border

From floral bouquet print, cut:
- 4 strips, the length of the fabric x $6\frac{1}{2}$" wide, for outer border (Strips are cut longer than necessary, and will be trimmed to size later.)

From green tonal, cut:
- 9 strips, $2\frac{1}{2}$" x 40", for double-fold binding

BLOCK ASSEMBLY

Organize your cut strips so all the #1 rectangles are in one pile, the #2 rectangles are in the next pile, etc. This is a really scrappy quilt, so the goal is to have as many different fabrics in each block as possible. Be sure to press your block after each step!

1. Begin by sewing a #1 rectangle to the right side of a red tonal 3" square.

2. Turn the unit to the left so the just-sewn #1 rectangle is on top and sew a #2 rectangle of a different print to the right-hand side.

3. Turn the unit to the left, so the just-sewn #2 rectangle is on top and add another #2 rectangle of a different print to the right-hand side.

4. Turn the unit to the left, so the just-sewn #2 rectangle is on top and add a #3 rectangle (again a different print) to the right-hand side.

5. Turn the unit to the left, so the just-sewn #3 rectangle is on top and add another #3 rectangle to the right-hand side.

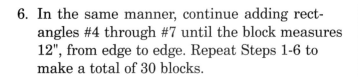

6. In the same manner, continue adding rectangles #4 through #7 until the block measures 12", from edge to edge. Repeat Steps 1-6 to make a total of 30 blocks.

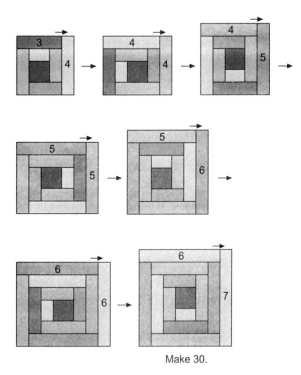

Make 30.

QUILT TOP ASSEMBLY

1. Following the Quilt Assembly Diagram at right, stitch the blocks together in 6 rows of 5 blocks each. Press seams in opposite directions from row to row.
2. Sew rows together as shown in the Quilt Assembly Diagram. Press seams in one direction.

BORDERS

1. Inner border: Sew the 7 red check inner border strips together, end-to-end, to make one long strip. Press seams open.
2. Measure length of quilt top through center. From the long strip, cut 2 red check inner border strips to this measurement, and sew to sides of quilt. Press seams toward border.
3. Measure width of quilt top, including borders just added, through center. From the long strip, cut 2 red check inner border strips to this measurement, and sew to top and bottom of quilt. Press seams toward border.

4. Outer border: Measure length of quilt top through center. Trim 2 floral bouquet outer border strips to this measurement, and sew to sides of quilt. Press seams toward outer border.
5. Measure width of quilt top, including borders just added, through center. Trim remaining 2 floral bouquet outer border strips to this measurement, and sew to top and bottom of quilt. Press seams toward outer border.

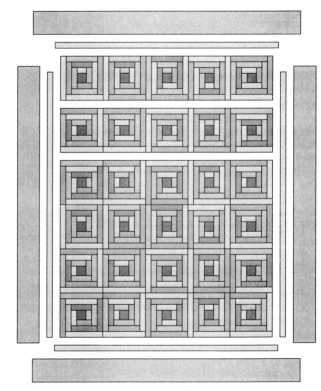

Quilt Assembly Diagram

See finishing instructions on pages 34-36.

Bumbleberry Baskets

Bumbleberry is the "scrap quilt" of pies. Imagine each basket in this quilt filled with different fruits: apples, peaches, berries, and even rhubarb. Mix all the fruits together to make a filling and you have Bumbleberry pie. It's our family favorite.

DESIGNED BY: Marsha McCloskey

QUILTED BY: Carrie Peterson

FINISHED QUILT SIZE: 44$\frac{1}{2}$" x 55"

FINISHED BLOCK SIZE: 7$\frac{1}{2}$" x 7$\frac{1}{2}$"

See this quilt in color in the center of the book.

Materials

Fabric requirements are based on Fat 8ths (useable measurement: 10" x 17"), or 40" fabric width.

- 12 Fat 8ths of assorted colored prints for baskets, ninepatches, and sashing units
- 12 Fat 8ths of assorted light-background prints for basket blocks, ninepatches, and sashing units
- $\frac{1}{3}$ yd. blue tonal print for inner border
- 2 yds. floral bouquet print for outer border and binding
- 3$\frac{3}{4}$ yds. for backing (lengthwise seam)
  OR 3$\frac{1}{8}$ yds. (widthwise seam)
- 53" x 63" batting

Directions

See *Quiltmaking Basics,* beginning on page 2, for general cutting and piecing directions. All cutting measurements include $\frac{1}{4}$"-wide seam allowance. Press seams in direction of arrows unless otherwise instructed. Templates are on page 13.

Basket block

Sashing unit

Ninepatch

CUTTING

When a number is followed by a second **number** in parentheses, the first number indicates the pieces needed to make one block or unit. The number in parentheses indicates the pieces needed to make all the blocks or units.

Study Fat 8th cutting diagram below and then, from Fat 8th assortment of 12 colored prints, cut:

- 1 (12) #3 baskets, for basket blocks (Basket template *does not* include seam allowance. You will need to add a seam allowance if you are using a traditional method of appliqué. See page 12.)
- 2 (62) #1 rectangles, 1½" x 8", for sashing units
- 4 (80) #2 squares, 1½" x 1½", for ninepatches

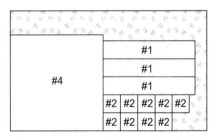

When cut as shown, 1 Fat 8th will yield 6 #1 rectangles, 7 #2 squares, and 1 #3 basket. Do this 12 times. You will have 10 extra #1 rectangles, and 4 extra #2 squares.

Study Fat 8th cutting diagram below and then, from Fat 8th assortment of 12 light-background prints, cut:

- 1 (12) #4 squares, 8" x 8", for basket blocks
- 1 (31) #1 rectangles, 1½" x 8", for sashing units
- 5 (100) #2 squares, 1½" x 1½", for ninepatches

When cut as shown, 1 Fat 8th will yield 1 #4 square, 3 #1 rectangles, and 9 #2 squares. Do this 12 times. You will have 5 extra #1 rectangles, and 8 extra #2 squares.

From blue tonal print, cut:
- 5 strips, 1¼" x 40", for inner border

From floral bouquet print, cut in order given:
- 6 strips, 2½" x 40", for double-fold binding
- 4 lengthwise strips, 50" x 4½" wide, for outer border (Strips are cut longer than necessary, and will be trimmed to size later.)

BLOCK ASSEMBLY

1. Using your favorite appliqué method or the one shown on page 12, appliqué the 12 colored print #3 basket shapes to the 12 light-background #4 squares. Six baskets tip to the right, and 6 baskets tip to the left. Edge-to-edge measurement of basket blocks should be 8".

Make 6.   Make 6.

2. Using 2 colored print #1 rectangles and 1 light-background #1 rectangle, assemble 1 sashing unit as shown. Edge-to-edge measurement of unit should be 3½" x 8". Repeat to make a total of 31 sashing units.

Make 31.

3. Using 4 colored print #2 squares, and 5 light-background #2 squares, assemble 1 ninepatch as shown. Edge-to-edge measurement of ninepatch should be 3½" x 3½". Repeat to make a total of 20 ninepatches.

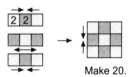

Make 20.

QUILT TOP ASSEMBLY

1. Using basket blocks, sashing units, and ninepatches, assemble rows as shown in the Quilt Assembly Diagram below. Press seams toward sashing units.
2. Sew rows together as shown in the Quilt Assembly Diagram. Press seams away from basket-block rows.

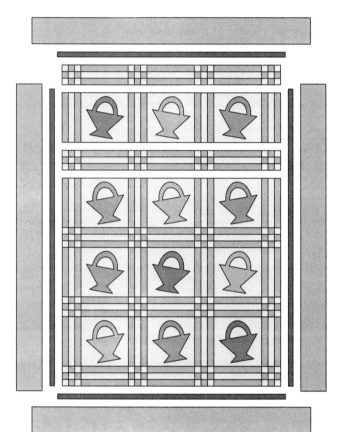

Quilt Assembly Diagram

BORDERS

1. Inner border: Sew 3 of the blue tonal inner border strips together, end-to-end, to make one long strip. Press seams open.
2. Measure length of quilt top through center. From the long strip, cut 2 blue tonal inner border strips to this measurement, and sew to sides of quilt. Press seams toward border.
3. Measure width of quilt top, including borders just added, through center. Trim remaining 2 blue tonal inner border strips to this measurement, and sew to top and bottom of quilt. Press seams toward border.
4. Outer border: Measure length of quilt top through center. Trim 2 floral bouquet outer border strips to this measurement, and sew to sides of quilt. Press seams toward outer border.
5. Measure width of quilt top, including borders just added, through center. Trim remaining 2 floral bouquet outer border strips to this measurement, and sew to top and bottom of quilt. Press seams toward outer border.

See finishing instructions on pages 34-36.

Paper Patch Appliqué

To make the baskets, you should use your favorite appliqué technique if you have one. The paper patch method described here is very traditional and works just fine.

1. You'll need a paper version of each basket to be appliquéd, so trace or photocopy 12 of basket template #3.

2. Pin each paper basket to the wrong side of the fabric and add a ¼" seam allowance as you cut around it. Clip inside curve of basket handle, and inner points.

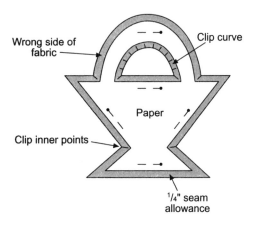

Wrong side of fabric

Clip curve

Paper

Clip inner points

¼" seam allowance

3. To prepare the baskets for appliqué, turn the seam allowance over the paper's edge, and baste the fabric to the paper.

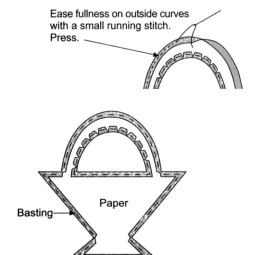

Ease fullness on outside curves with a small running stitch. Press.

Paper

Basting

4. Position a basket on a #4 background square and pin in place. The basket should be tipped slightly to the right or left. Study the photograph of the Bumbleberry Baskets quilt in the center of the book, and approximate the angle shown in that quilt. Don't worry about the angle being exact! This is a fun quilt, and some variation in basket angles adds to the charm.

5. Leaving the paper in place, appliqué the basket to the background square. Use thread the same color as the basket. Stitch the basket in place by hand, using a blind stitch; or by machine, using a shallow zigzag stitch.

6. After the basket is stitched in place, remove the basting stitches.

7. To remove the paper, turn the block to the wrong side and carefully cut away the background fabric behind the basket, leaving a ¼" seam allowance. Pull out the paper from the back. Press.

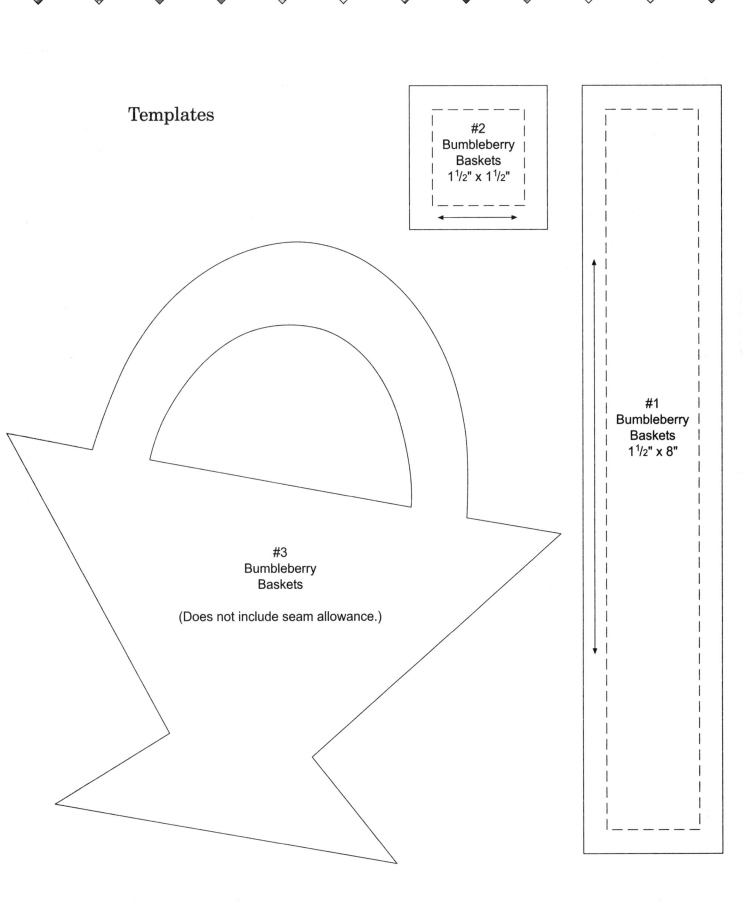

Templates

#2
Bumbleberry
Baskets
$1\frac{1}{2}$" x $1\frac{1}{2}$"

#1
Bumbleberry
Baskets
$1\frac{1}{2}$" x 8"

#3
Bumbleberry
Baskets

(Does not include seam allowance.)

Peaches and Cream

The traditional name for this pattern is Birds in the Air. It's a great design for perfecting your triangle piecing.

DESIGNED BY: Marsha McCloskey

QUILTED BY: Carrie Peterson

FINISHED QUILT SIZE: 41" x 50"

FINISHED BLOCK SIZE: $4^1/2$" x $4^1/2$"

See this quilt in color in the center of the book.

Materials

Fabric requirements are based on Fat 8ths (useable measurement: 10" x 17"), or 40" fabric width.

- 8 Fat 8ths of assorted colored prints for blocks
- 8 Fat 8ths of assorted light-background prints for blocks
- $1^1/2$ yds. Fat 8ths panel stripe peach-and-green print for border (On the "panel stripe" prints, four different designs are printed lengthwise on a single piece of fabric.)
  OR $1^1/2$ yds. of one print
- $1/2$ yd. green check for binding
- $3^3/8$ yds. for backing (lengthwise seam)
  OR $2^7/8$ yds. (widthwise seam)
- 49" x 58" batting

Directions

See *Quiltmaking Basics,* beginning on page 2, for general cutting and piecing directions. All cutting measurements include $1/4$"-wide seam allowance. Press seams in direction of arrows unless otherwise instructed. Templates are on page 16.

Block A

Block B

CUTTING

When a number is followed by a second number in parentheses, the first number indicates the pieces needed to make one block. The number in parentheses indicates the pieces needed to make all the blocks.

Study Fat 8th cutting diagram below and then, from Fat 8th assortment of 8 colored prints, cut:

- 1 (16) squares, $5^3/8$" x $5^3/8$"; cut each square once diagonally to make 2 (32) #1 triangles for A blocks (one extra)
- 2 (68) squares, $3^1/8$" x $3^1/8$"; cut each square once diagonally to make 4 (136) #2 triangles for B blocks.

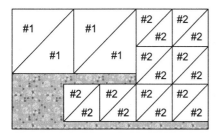

When cut as shown, 1 Fat 8th will yield 4 #1 triangles, and 16 #2 triangles. Do this 8 times. There will be 1 extra #1 triangle, and enough fabric left over to cut 8 more #2 triangles for the corner blocks in the borders.

Study Fat 8th cutting diagram below and then, from Fat 8th assortment of 8 light-background prints, cut:

- 1 (16) squares, $5^3/8$" x $5^3/8$"; cut each square once diagonally to make 2 (32) #1 triangles for A blocks (one extra)
- 2 (68) squares, $3^1/8$" x $3^1/8$"; cut each square once diagonally to make 4 (136) #2 triangles for B blocks.

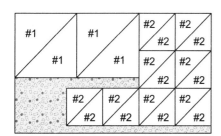

When cut as shown, 1 Fat 8th will yield 4 #1 triangles, and 16 #2 triangles. Do this 8 times. There will be 1 extra #1 triangle, and enough fabric left over to cut 8 more #2 triangles for the corner blocks in the borders.

From Fat 8th panel stripe peach-and-green print, or from single print, cut:

- 4 strips, 5" x length of fabric*, for border (If using panel stripe, cut 1 strip from each of the 4 different designs.)

From green check, cut:

- 5 strips, $2^1/2$" x 40", for double-fold binding

*Strips are cut longer than necessary, and will be trimmed to size later.

Accuracy Test

When you sew two triangles together to make a square, check the size of the square to make sure you have sewn the proper $1/4$" seam allowance. Two #1 triangles sewn together should make a square that measures 5" x 5", edge to edge. Two #2 triangles sewn together should make a square that measures $2^3/4$" x $2^3/4$", edge to edge.

BLOCK ASSEMBLY

1. Using 1 colored print #1 triangle, and 1 light-background #1 triangle, assemble 1 Block A as shown. Edge-to-edge measurement of block should be 5" x 5". Repeat to make a total of 31 blocks.

Block A
Make 31.

2. Using 4 colored print #2 triangles, and 4 light-background #2 triangles, assemble 1 Block B as shown. Edge-to-edge measurement of block should be 5" x 5". Repeat to make a total of 34 blocks. (In the sample quilt, 32 of the B blocks are made using two different prints each; the 2 corner blocks are scrappier.)

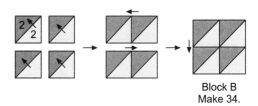

Block B
Make 34.

QUILT TOP ASSEMBLY

1. Following the Quilt Assembly Diagram below, stitch the blocks together in 9 rows of 7 blocks each, alternating the A and B blocks. Press seams toward A blocks. (Set aside 2 B blocks to be used for border corners.)
2. Sew rows together as shown in the Quilt Assembly Diagram. Press seams in one direction.

BORDERS

1. Measure length of quilt top through center. Cut 2 peach-and-green border strips to this measurement, and sew to sides of quilt. Press seams toward border.

2. Following the Quilt Assembly Diagram for placement, sew 1 Block B to the end of each of the remaining 2 peach-and-green border strips. Press seams toward border strips.
3. Measure width of quilt top, including borders just added, through center. Trim 2 peach-and-green border strips (with B blocks) to this measurement, and sew to top and bottom of quilt. Press seams toward border.

See finishing instructions on pages 34-36.

Templates

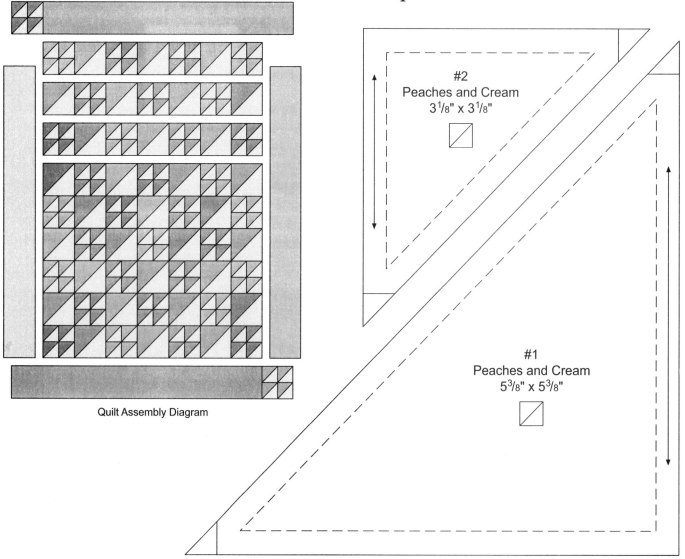

Quilt Assembly Diagram

#2
Peaches and Cream
3$\frac{1}{8}$" x 3$\frac{1}{8}$"

#1
Peaches and Cream
5$\frac{3}{8}$" x 5$\frac{3}{8}$"

Peaches and Cream

Bumbleberry Baskets

Out to Sea

Spring Fancy

Spring Fancy

The traditional name for this pieced block is Rabbit's Paw. It's simple to piece, and the bright pink triangles form a secondary "star" where the block corners meet the sashing and cornerstones.

DESIGNED BY: Marsha McCloskey

QUILTED BY: Carrie Peterson

FINISHED QUILT SIZE: 53" x 63½"

FINISHED BLOCK SIZE: 9" x 9"

See this quilt in color in the center of the book.

Materials

Fabric requirements are based on Fat 8ths (useable measurement: 10" x 17"), or 40" fabric width.

- 8 Fat 8ths of assorted green prints for blocks
- ½ yd. pink tonal for blocks
- 1⅝ yds. light-background print for blocks
- ¾ yd. green tonal for cornerstones and binding
- 1 yd. green check for sashing
- 1¾ yds. floral bouquet print for border
- 4¼ yds. for backing (lengthwise seam)
  OR 3⅝ yds. (widthwise seam)
- 61" x 72" batting

Directions

See *Quiltmaking Basics,* beginning on page 2, for general cutting and piecing directions. All cutting measurements include ¼"-wide seam allowance. Press seams in direction of arrows unless otherwise instructed. Templates are on page 23.

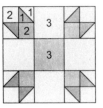

CUTTING

When a number is followed by a second number in parentheses, the first number indicates the pieces needed to make one block. The number in parentheses indicates the pieces needed to make all 20 blocks.

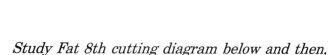

Study Fat 8th cutting diagram below and then, from Fat 8th assortment of 8 green prints, cut:
- 4 (80) #2 squares, 2" x 2", for blocks
- 1 (20) #3 squares, $3^1/2$" x $3^1/2$", for blocks

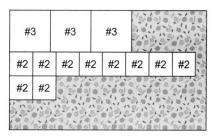

When cut as shown, 1 Fat 8th will yield 3 #3 squares, and 10 #2 squares. Do this 8 times. You will have 4 extra #3 squares.

From pink tonal, cut:
- 4 (80) squares, $2^3/8$" x $2^3/8$"; cut each square once diagonally to make 8 (160) #1 triangles for blocks

From light-background print, cut:
- 4 (80) #3 squares, $3^1/2$" x $3^1/2$", for blocks
- 4 (80) squares, $2^3/8$" x $2^3/8$"; cut each square once diagonally to make 8 (160) #1 triangles for blocks
- 4 (80) #2 squares, 2" x 2", for blocks

From green tonal, cut in order given:
- 7 strips, $2^1/2$" x 40", for double-fold binding
- 30 #2 squares, 2" x 2", for cornerstones

From green check, cut:
- 49 rectangles, 2" x $9^1/2$", for sashing

From floral bouquet, cut:
- 4 strips, the length of the fabric x 5" wide, for border

BLOCK ASSEMBLY
1. Sew 8 pink tonal #1 triangles and 8 light-background #1 triangles together in pairs to make 8 triangle units.

Make 8.

2. Join two of the triangle units with 1 green #2 square, and 1 light-background #2 square, to make a corner unit. Repeat to make 4 corner units.

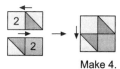

Make 4.

3. Join corner units together with 1 green #3 square, and 4 light-background #3 squares as shown to make a block. Edge-to-edge measurement of block should be $9^1/2$" x $9^1/2$". Repeat Steps 1-3 to make a total of 20 blocks.

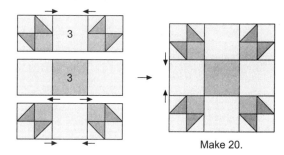

Make 20.

QUILT TOP ASSEMBLY
1. Following the Quilt Assembly Diagram on page 23, stitch blocks, sashing rectangles, and cornerstone squares together in rows. Press seams toward sashing rectangles.
2. Sew rows together as shown in the Quilt Assembly Diagram. Press seams toward sashing rows.

BORDERS
1. Measure length of quilt top through center. Trim 2 floral bouquet border strips to this measurement, and sew to sides of quilt. Press seams toward border.
2. Measure width of quilt top, including borders just added, through center. Trim remaining 2 floral bouquet border strips to this measurement, and sew to top and bottom of quilt. Press seams toward border.

See finishing instructions on pages 34-36.

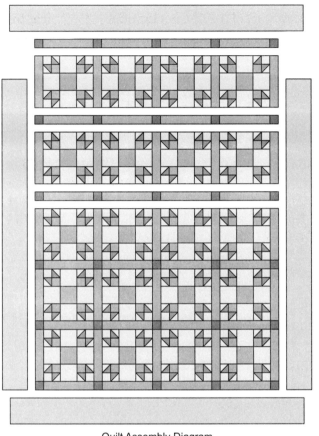

Quilt Assembly Diagram

Templates

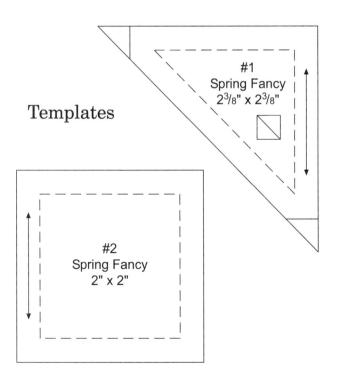

#1
Spring Fancy
$2^3/_8$" x $2^3/_8$"

#2
Spring Fancy
2" x 2"

#3
Spring Fancy
$3^1/_2$" x $3^1/_2$"

Out to Sea

This quilt reminds me of the slightly chaotic, weekly sailing event called the Duck Dodge on Lake Union in Seattle: a lot of little sailboats going every which way. Ducks beware!

DESIGNED BY: Marsha McCloskey

QUILTED BY: Carrie Peterson

FINISHED QUILT SIZE: 46$^{1}/_{2}$" x 51$^{1}/_{2}$"

FINISHED SAILBOAT BLOCK SIZE: 8" x 6"

FINISHED WAVE BLOCK SIZE: 4" x 6"

See this quilt in color in the center of the book.

Materials

Fabric requirements are based on Fat 8ths (useable measurement: 10" x 17"), or 40" fabric width.

- 8 Fat 8ths of assorted bright prints for blocks
- 12 Fat 8ths of assorted light-background prints for blocks
- 1$^{3}/_{4}$ yds. blue check for sashing, inner border, and middle strip of backing
- 1$^{3}/_{8}$ yds. blue tonal for outer border
- $^{5}/_{8}$ yd. red tonal for binding
- 1$^{3}/_{4}$ yds. for backing
- 55" x 60" batting

Directions

See *Quiltmaking Basics,* beginning on page 2, for general cutting and piecing directions. All cutting measurements include $^{1}/_{4}$"-wide seam allowance. Press seams in direction of arrows unless otherwise instructed. Templates are on page 27.

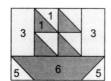

Sailboat block

Wave block

Square-in-a-Square block

CUTTING

When a number is followed by a second number in parentheses, the first number indicates the pieces needed to make one block. The number in parentheses indicates the pieces needed to make all blocks.

Study Fat 8th cutting diagrams below and then, from Fat 8th assortment of 8 bright prints, cut a total of:

- 1 (18) #6 rectangles, $2^1/2$" x $8^1/2$", for Sailboat blocks (Stitch-and-flip technique will be used.)
- 2 (36) squares, $2^7/8$" x $2^7/8$"; cut each square once diagonally to make 4 (72) #1 triangles for Sailboat blocks
- 2 (36) squares, $1^7/8$" x $1^7/8$"; cut each square once diagonally to make 4 (72) #2 triangles for Wave blocks
- 4 (16) #5 squares, $2^1/2$" x $2^1/2$", for Square-in-a-Square blocks (Stitch-and-flip technique will be used.)

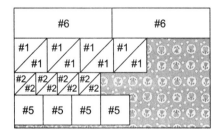

When cut as shown, 1 Fat 8th will yield 2 #6 rectangles, 8 #1 triangles, 8 #2 triangles, and 4 #5 squares. Do this 4 times, then do 2 more times without the #5 squares.

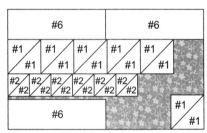

When cut as shown, 1 Fat 8th will yield 3 #6 rectangles, 12 #1 triangles, and 12 #2 triangles. Do this 2 times.

Study Fat 8th cutting diagrams at right and then, from Fat 8th assortment of 12 light-background prints, cut a total of:

- 1 (18) #4 rectangles, $4^1/2$" x $5^1/2$", for Wave blocks
- 1 (4) #7 squares, $4^1/2$" x $4^1/2$", for Square-in-a-Square blocks (Stitch-and-flip technique will be used.)
- 2 (36) #3 rectangles, $2^1/2$" x $4^1/2$", for Sailboat blocks

- 2 (36) squares, $2^7/8$" x $2^7/8$"; cut each square once diagonally to make 4 (72) #1 triangles for Sailboat blocks
- 2 (36) #5 squares, $2^1/2$" x $2^1/2$", for Sailboat blocks (Stitch-and-flip technique will be used.)
- 2 (36) squares, $1^7/8$" x $1^7/8$"; cut each square once diagonally to make 4 (72) #2 triangles for Wave blocks

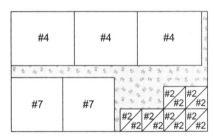

When cut as shown, 1 Fat 8th will yield 4 #3 rectangles, 4 #5 squares, 4 #2 triangles, 1 #4 rectangle, and 8 #1 triangles. Do this 9 times.

When cut as shown, 1 Fat 8th will yield 3 #4 rectangles, 2 #7 squares, and 12 #2 triangles. Do this 3 times. You will have 2 extra #7 squares.

From blue check, cut:

- 9 strips, the length of fabric x $1^1/2$" wide, for sashing and inner border (Strips are cut longer than necessary, and will be trimmed to size later.)
- 1 strip, the length of fabric x approximately 18" wide (Set aside to be used as the center panel of the quilt backing.)

From blue tonal, cut:

- 4 strips, the length of fabric x $4^1/2$" wide, for outer border (Strips are cut longer than necessary, and will be trimmed to size later.)

From red tonal, cut:

- 6 strips, $2^1/2$" x 40", for double-fold binding

BLOCK ASSEMBLY

Note: Before assembling blocks, refer to the photo in the Quilt Gallery in the center of the book for color placement. Note that 9 sailboats are sailing east, and 9 are sailing west.

1. Using a pencil, draw a diagonal line, from corner to corner, on the wrong side of 36 light-background #5 squares.

2. With right sides together, place a marked #5 square at one end of a bright #6 rectangle. Sew on the drawn line. Trim as shown, leaving a $1/4$" seam allowance. Press seam toward rectangle. Repeat step on opposite end of rectangle. Make 18 of these boat hull units.

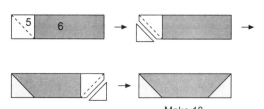

Make 18.

3. Assemble a Sailboat block using 1 boat hull unit, 4 bright #1 triangles, 4 light-background #1 triangles, and 2 light-background #3 rectangles as shown. Edge-to-edge measurement of block should be $8^1/2$" x $6^1/2$". Repeat to make a total of 9 westbound and 9 eastbound Sailboat blocks.

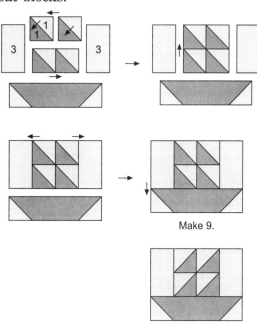

Make 9.

Make 9.

4. Assemble a Wave block using 4 bright #2 triangles, 4 light-background #2 triangles, and 1 light-background #4 rectangle as shown. Edge-to-edge measurement of block should be $4^1/2$" x $6^1/2$". Repeat to make a total of 9 west-bound and 9 eastbound Wave blocks.

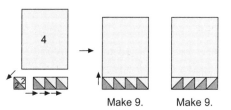

Make 9. Make 9.

5. Using a pencil, draw a diagonal line, from corner to corner, on the wrong side of 16 bright #5 squares.

6. With right sides together, place one marked #5 square on a corner of a light-background #7 square. Sew on the drawn line. Trim as shown, leaving a $1/4$" seam allowance. Press seam toward triangle. Repeat step on remaining 3 corners of the square. Edge-to-edge measurement of block should be $4^1/2$" x $4^1/2$". Make 4 of these Square-in-a-Square blocks.

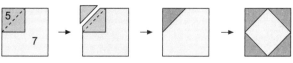

Make 4.

QUILT TOP ASSEMBLY

1. Following the Quilt Assembly Diagram on page 27, sew the Sailboat and Wave blocks together in rows. Press seams toward Wave blocks.

2. Measure the length of the rows (they should be approximately $36^1/2$"). If all 6 rows do not measure the same, take an average of the 6 measurements. Cut 7 of the $1^1/2$"-wide blue check strips to this measurement.

3. Sew block rows and blue check strips together as shown in the Quilt Assembly Diagram. Press seams toward blue check strips.
4. Measure length of quilt top through center. Trim the remaining 2 blue check strips to this measurement, and sew to sides of quilt. Press seams toward blue check strips.

BORDERS

1. Measure width of quilt top through center. Trim 2 blue tonal outer border strips to this measurement. Sew a Square-in-a-Square block to each end of the 2 strips as shown in the Quilt Assembly Diagram. Press seams toward border strips. Set these border strips aside until Step 3.
2. Measure length of quilt top through center. Trim remaining 2 blue tonal outer border strips to this measurement, and sew to sides of quilt. Press seams toward outer border.
3. Sew the border strips made in Step 1 to top and bottom of quilt. Press seams toward outer border.

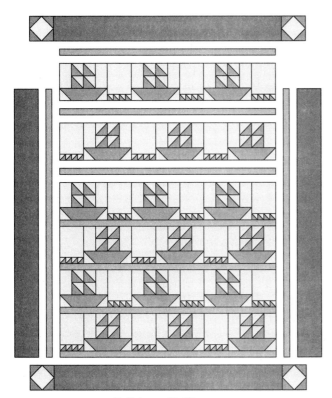

Quilt Assembly Diagram

BACKING

Cut the 1$\frac{3}{4}$ yards backing fabric lengthwise down the center to make 2 long panels. Sew 1 of these panels on each side of the blue check panel (which was set aside for this purpose) to complete your quilt backing.

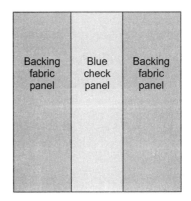

See finishing instructions on pages 34-36.

Templates

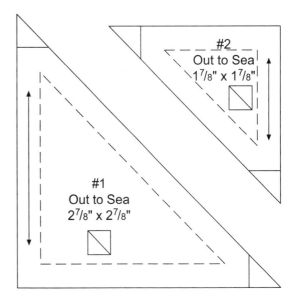

#2
Out to Sea
1$\frac{7}{8}$" x 1$\frac{7}{8}$"

#1
Out to Sea
2$\frac{7}{8}$" x 2$\frac{7}{8}$"

Tulips in Bloom

A trip to the tulip fields around La Conner, Washington, inspired this quilt. In a field all the tulips are the same color, yet each bloom is slightly different.

DESIGNED BY: Marsha McCloskey

QUILTED BY: Sheila Snyder

FINISHED QUILT SIZE: $54\frac{1}{2}$" x $69\frac{1}{2}$"

FINISHED BLOCK SIZE: 8" x 9"

See this quilt in color on the inside back cover.

Materials

Fabric requirements are based on Fat 8ths (**useable measurement: 10" x 17"**), or 40" fabric width.

- 4 Fat 8ths of assorted green prints for blocks
- 4 Fat 8ths of assorted lavender prints for blocks
- 4 Fat 8ths of assorted purple prints for star points
- 20 Fat 8ths of assorted light-background prints for blocks and sashing
- 1 Fat 8th pink tonal for square in tulip blocks
- 1 Fat 8th yellow tonal for star centers
- $\frac{1}{2}$ yd. light print for inner border
- 1 yd. green tonal for middle border and binding
- $1\frac{7}{8}$ yds. Fat 8ths panel stripe green print for outer border and blocks (On the "panel stripe" prints, four different designs are printed lengthwise on a single piece of fabric.) OR $1\frac{7}{8}$ yds. of one print
- $4\frac{1}{2}$ yds. for backing (lengthwise seam) OR $3\frac{3}{4}$ yds. (widthwise seam)
- 63" x 78" batting

Directions

See *Quiltmaking Basics,* beginning on page 2, for general cutting and piecing directions. All cutting measurements include $\frac{1}{4}$"-wide seam allowance. Press seams in direction of arrows unless otherwise instructed. Templates are on page 33.

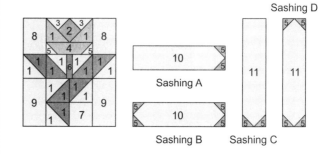

CUTTING

When a number is followed by a second number in parentheses, the first number indicates the pieces needed to make one block. The number in parentheses indicates the pieces needed to make all 20 blocks.

From Fat 8th panel stripe green print, or from single print, cut *in order given*:

- 4 strips, 5" x length of fabric, for outer border (If using panel stripe, cut 1 strip from each of the 4 different designs. Strips are cut longer than necessary, and will be trimmed to size later.)
- 30 squares, $2^7/8$" x $2^7/8$"; cut each square once diagonally to make 60 #1 triangles (7 are needed for each block; more will be cut from green Fat 8ths below.)
- 12 #6 rectangles, 1" x $2^1/2$", for tulip stems (1 is needed for each block; more will be cut from green Fat 8ths below.)

Study Fat 8th cutting diagram below and then, from Fat 8th assortment of 4 green prints, cut:

- 40 squares, $2^7/8$" x $2^7/8$"; cut each square once diagonally to make 80 #1 triangles (7 are needed for each block.)
- 8 #6 rectangles, 1" x $2^1/2$", for tulip stems (1 is needed for each block.)

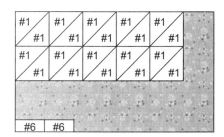

When cut as shown, 1 Fat 8th will yield 20 #1 triangles, and 2 #6 rectangles. Do this 4 times.

From Fat 8th assortment of 4 lavender prints, cut:

- 1 (20) squares, $2^7/8$" x $2^7/8$"; cut each square once diagonally to make 2 (40) #1 triangles for blocks
- 1 (20) #4 rectangles, $1^1/2$" x $4^1/2$", for blocks*

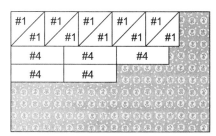

When cut as shown, 1 Fat 8th will yield 10 #1 triangles, and 5 #4 rectangles. Do this 4 times.

From Fat 8th assortment of 4 purple prints, cut:

- 96 #5 squares, $1^1/2$" x $1^1/2$", for star points in sashing units*

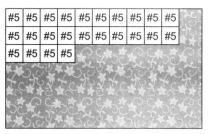

When cut as shown, 1 Fat 8th will yield 24 #5 squares. Do this 4 times.

From Fat 8th assortment of 20 light-background prints, cut:

- 4 (80) squares, $2^7/8$" x $2^7/8$"; cut each square once diagonally to make 8 (160) #1 triangles (7 are needed for each block.)
- 1 (20) squares, $3^1/4$" x $3^1/4$"; cut each square twice diagonally to make 4 (80) #3 triangles (2 are needed for each block.)
- 2 (40) #5 squares, $1^1/2$" x $1^1/2$", for blocks*
- 1 (20) #7 squares, $2^1/2$" x $2^1/2$", for blocks
- 2 (40) #8 rectangles, $2^1/2$" x $3^1/2$", for blocks
- 2 (40) #9 rectangles, $2^1/2$" x $4^1/2$", for blocks
- 16 #10 rectangles, $2^1/2$" x $8^1/2$", for A and B sashing units*
- 15 #11 rectangles, $2^1/2$" x $9^1/2$", for C and D sashing units*

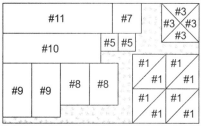

When cut as shown, 1 Fat 8th will yield 8 #1 triangles, 4 #3 triangles, 2 #5 squares, 1 #7 square, 2 #8 rectangles, 2 #9 rectangles, 1 #10 rectangle, and 1 #11 rectangle. Do this 20 times. You will have extra #1 and #3 triangles. (You can stop cutting the #10 and #11 rectangles when you have 16 of #10 and 15 of #11.)

*Stitch-and-flip technique will be used.

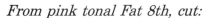

From pink tonal Fat 8th, cut:
- 1 (20) #2 squares, $1^{15}/_{16}$" x $1^{15}/_{16}$", for blocks

From yellow tonal Fat 8th, cut:
- 12 squares, $2^{1}/_{2}$" x $2^{1}/_{2}$", for star centers (sashing cornerstones)

From light print, cut:
- 5 strips, $2^{1}/_{2}$" x 40", for inner border

From green tonal, cut:
- 6 strips, 2" x 40", for middle border
- 7 strips, $2^{1}/_{2}$" x 40", for double-fold binding

BLOCK ASSEMBLY

1. Using a pencil, draw a diagonal line, from corner to corner, on the wrong side of 40 light-background #5 squares.

2. With right sides together, place one of the marked #5 squares at one end of a lavender #4 rectangle. Sew on the drawn line. Trim as shown, leaving a $1/_{4}$" seam allowance. Press seam toward rectangle. Repeat step on opposite end of rectangle. Make 20 of these units.

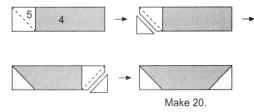

Make 20.

3. Assemble the upper portion of a Tulip block using a unit made in Step 2, 2 lavender #1 triangles, 1 pink #2 square, 2 light-background #3 triangles, and 2 light-background #8 rectangles. Repeat to make a total of 20 of these upper-block units.

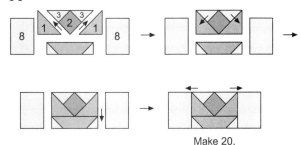

Make 20.

4. Sew together a green #1 triangle and a light-background #1 triangle. Repeat to make a total of 140 of these triangle units.

Make 140.

5. Arrange 2 triangle units as shown. Trim $1/_{4}$" off the inside edge of each triangle unit, then sew the units to each side of a green #6 rectangle. Edge-to-edge measurement of unit should be $2^{1}/_{2}$" x $4^{1}/_{2}$". Repeat to make a total of 20 of these stem units.

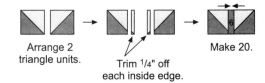

Arrange 2 triangle units.

Trim $1/_{4}$" off each inside edge.

Make 20.

6. Assemble the lower portion of a Tulip block using a stem unit, 5 triangle units, 1 light-background #7 square, and 2 light-background #9 rectangles as shown. Repeat to make a total of 20 of these lower-block units.

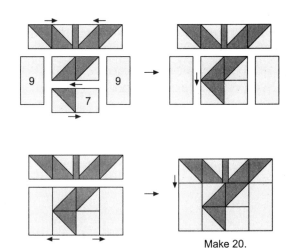

Make 20.

7. Make 20 Tulip blocks by sewing upper-block and lower-block units together. Edge-to-edge measurement of block should be $8^{1}/_{2}"$ x $9^{1}/_{2}"$. Repeat to make a total of 20 Tulip blocks.

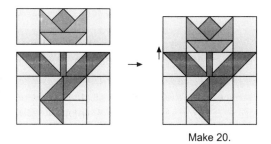

Make 20.

SASHING UNIT ASSEMBLY

1. Using a pencil, draw a diagonal line, from corner to corner, on the wrong side of 96 purple #5 squares.

2. With right sides together, place one of the marked #5 squares on the upper right corner of a light-background #10 rectangle. Sew on the drawn line. Trim as shown, leaving a $^{1}/_{4}"$ seam allowance. Press seam toward triangle. Repeat step on lower right corner. Edge-to-edge measurement of unit should be $2^{1}/_{2}"$ x $8^{1}/_{2}"$. Make 8 of these Sashing A units.

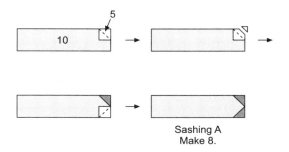

Sashing A
Make 8.

3. With right sides together, place one of the marked #5 squares on a corner of a light-background #10 rectangle. Sew on the drawn line. Trim as shown, leaving a $^{1}/_{4}"$ seam allowance. Press seam toward triangle. Repeat step on remaining 3 corners. Edge-to-edge measurement of unit should be $2^{1}/_{2}"$ x $8^{1}/_{2}"$. Make 8 of these Sashing B units.

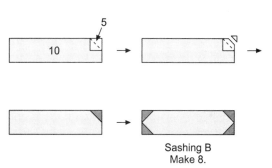

Sashing B
Make 8.

4. With right sides together, place one of the marked #5 squares on the upper right corner of a light-background #11 rectangle. Sew on the drawn line. Trim as shown, leaving a $^{1}/_{4}"$ seam allowance. Press seam toward triangle. Repeat step on lower right corner. Edge-to-edge measurement of unit should be $2^{1}/_{2}"$ x $9^{1}/_{2}"$. Make 6 of these Sashing C units.

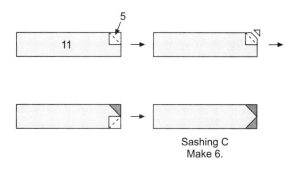

Sashing C
Make 6.

5. With right sides together, place one of the marked #5 squares on a corner of a light-background #11 rectangle. Sew on the drawn line. Trim as shown, leaving a $1/4$" seam allowance. Press seam toward triangle. Repeat step on remaining 3 corners. Edge-to-edge measurement of unit should be $2^{1}/_{2}$" x $9^{1}/_{2}$". Make 9 of these Sashing D units.

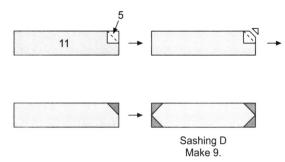

Sashing D
Make 9.

QUILT TOP ASSEMBLY

Note: In assembling your quilt top, pay particular attention to the placement of the sashing units. For reference, use the photo on the inside back cover and the Quilt Assembly Diagram at right.

1. Following the Quilt Assembly Diagram, sew the Tulip blocks, Sashing units, and 12 yellow tonal $2^{1}/_{2}$" squares together in rows. Press seams away from Sashing units.
2. Sew rows together as shown in the Quilt Assembly Diagram. Press seams toward sashing rows.

BORDERS

1. Inner border: Sew the 5 light print inner border strips together, end-to-end, to make one long strip. Press seams open.
2. Measure length of quilt top through center. From the long strip, cut 2 light print inner border strips to this measurement, and sew to sides of quilt. Press seams toward border.
3. Measure width of quilt top, including borders just added, through center. From the long strip, cut 2 light print inner border strips to this measurement, and sew to top and bottom of quilt. Press seams toward border.
4. Middle border: Repeat Steps 1-3, using 6 green tonal 2" strips.

5. Outer border: Measure length of quilt top through center. Trim 2 green print outer border strips to this measurement, and sew to sides of quilt. Press seams toward outer border.
6. Measure width of quilt top, including borders just added, through center. Trim remaining 2 green print outer border strips to this measurement, and sew to top and bottom of quilt. Press seams toward outer border.

See finishing instructions on pages 34-36.

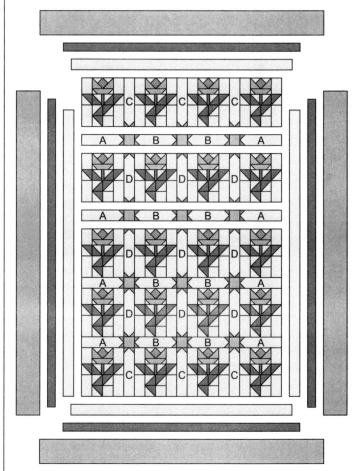

Quilt Assembly Diagram

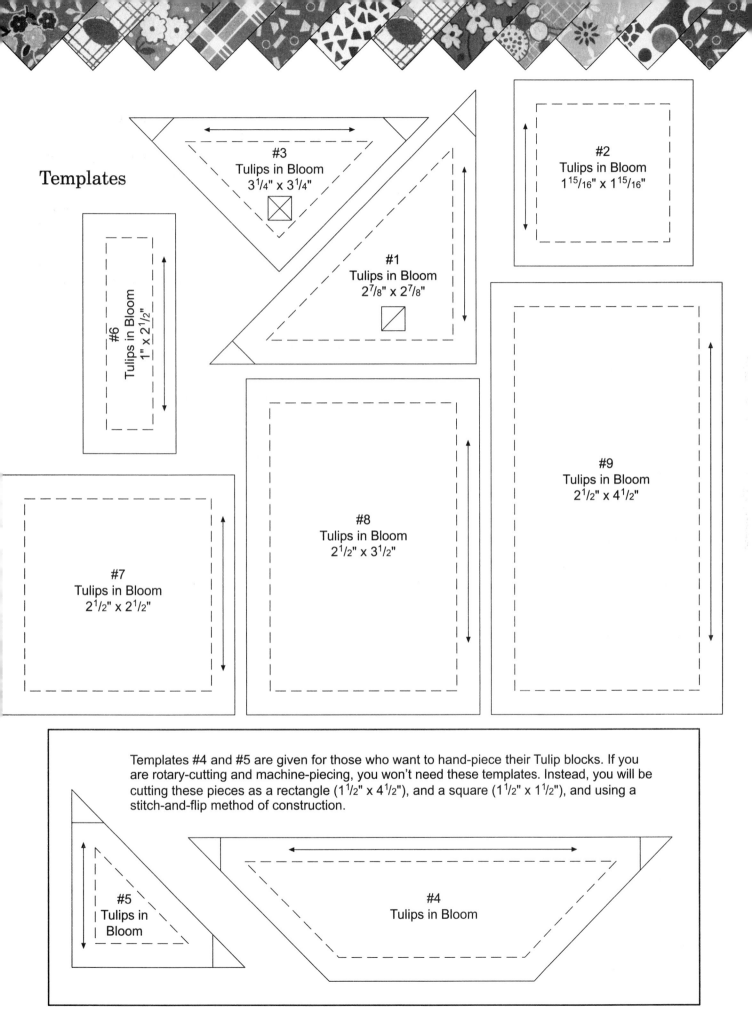

Templates

#3
Tulips in Bloom
3¼" x 3¼"

#2
Tulips in Bloom
1¹⁵⁄₁₆" x 1¹⁵⁄₁₆"

#1
Tulips in Bloom
2⁷⁄₈" x 2⁷⁄₈"

#6
Tulips in Bloom
1" x 2½"

#9
Tulips in Bloom
2½" x 4½"

#8
Tulips in Bloom
2½" x 3½"

#7
Tulips in Bloom
2½" x 2½"

Templates #4 and #5 are given for those who want to hand-piece their Tulip blocks. If you are rotary-cutting and machine-piecing, you won't need these templates. Instead, you will be cutting these pieces as a rectangle (1½" x 4½"), and a square (1½" x 1½"), and using a stitch-and-flip method of construction.

#5
Tulips in Bloom

#4
Tulips in Bloom

Quiltmaking Basics

Making Your Quilt Top

Setting the Quilt Blocks Together

When the design blocks and setting pieces (large squares, triangles and/or sashing strips) are sewn together to make a quilt top, it is called the "set." Each quilt pattern has a Quilt Assembly Diagram showing how the parts will be sewn together in rows. When sewing the rows together, press for opposing seams and pin all points of matching.

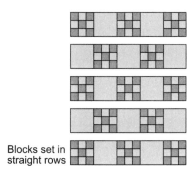

Blocks set in straight rows

Borders

The borders for the quilts in this book are made of strips of fabric sewn to the sides and then to the top and bottom edges of the quilt top. Some of the borders have pieced blocks at the corners.

To cut the two side borders to the right length, measure the quilt top length (including seam allowances) through the center, as shown in diagram at right. (On large quilts, it's a good idea to measure the length along both outer edges as well and use the average of the three measurements.) Cut the two border strips this length. Mark the center and quarter points on both the quilt top and border strips. Matching ends, centers, and quarter points, pin border strips to the quilt top. Pin generously and press along the matched edges to set the seam before sewing. A shot of steam will help with any easing that might be required.

Using a ¼" seam allowance, stitch the border to the quilt top. Press the seam allowance to one

side as directed in the quilt instructions. For the top and bottom borders, measure the quilt width, including the borders just added. Cut the strips, then pin and sew them to the top and bottom of the quilt. (When applicable, border details – such as adding corner blocks – are included in the instructions for each quilt.)

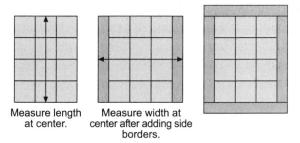

Measure length at center.

Measure width at center after adding side borders.

Finishing Your Quilt

Plan and Mark Quilting Designs

The fabrics used in *More Fat 8ths and Friends* make a lively quilt surface in design and color. All of our quilts were quilted by machine, with simple designs chosen to enhance the fresh look and feel of each quilt.

In choosing your own quilting designs, remember that quilting lines should be evenly distributed over the quilt surface. Directions that come with your batting will tell how close the quilting lines must be to keep the batting from coming apart when the quilt is washed. Avoid tight complicated designs that then require similar quilting over the whole quilt. Likewise avoid leaving large areas unquilted.

Some quilters prefer to mark their quilt top with quilting lines before it is assembled with the backing and batting. To do this, you will need marking pencils, a long ruler or yardstick; stencils or templates for quilting motifs; and a smooth, clean, hard surface on which to work. Thoroughly press the quilt top. Use a sharp marking pencil and lightly mark the quilting lines on the fabric. No matter what kind of marking tool you use, light lines will be easier to remove than heavy ones.

Backing and Batting

Prepare the backing. For quilts that measure more than 38" wide, you will need to make the backing by cutting and sewing two or more lengths of fabric together. Add 8" to the length and width of the completed quilt top for a working allowance (4" all the way around).

To make a backing that is large enough, cut lengths of fabric and sew them together on the long sides. Press the seams open. You can sew two lengths together with one center seam, or split the second length and sew the pieces to each side of the other length of fabric. Sometimes, to save fabric, it is best to cut and piece the backing so the seam runs across the width of the quilt.

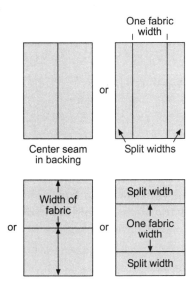

Choose a thin cotton or cotton-polyester blend batting in a size that is longer and wider than your quilt top. Trim batting to size of backing.

Layering the Quilt

Lay the backing face down on a large, clean, flat surface – the floor or a large table. With masking tape, tape the backing down to keep it smooth and flat while you are working with the other layers. If you are working on a table, part of the quilt will probably hang over the sides. Begin in the quilt center and work in sections toward the sides and ends. Gently lay the batting on top of the backing, centering and smoothing it as you go. Center the freshly ironed quilt top on top of

the batting, right side up. Starting in the middle, gently smooth out fullness to the sides and corners. Take care not to distort the straight lines of the quilt design and the borders.

Baste the layers together with safety pins or needle and light-colored thread. Start in the middle and make a line of long stitches to each corner to form a large X. Continue basting in a grid of parallel lines 6"-8" apart. Finish with a row of basting around the outside edges – $1/4$" away from the edge.

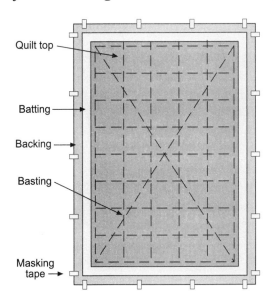

Quilting

Quilt the layers together by hand or machine. This is a little sentence to cover a big subject. There are whole books written on how to quilt. There are also many professional longarm-machine-quilters who will do the quilting for you. Before you decide on a quilting method, consider how you will be using your quilt. Will it be a rarely-used heirloom quilt, or do you plan to use the quilt daily? Heirloom quilts are often enhanced by hand-quilting. Everyday quilts may be better served by quick and durable machine quilting.

Binding

After quilting, trim excess batting and backing even with the edge of the quilt top. A rotary cutter and long ruler will ensure accurate straight edges. If basting is no longer in place, machine-baste all three layers of the quilt together close to the edge.

In the cutting instructions for each quilt, you will find the number of $2^{1}/_{2}$" x 40" strips needed to bind that quilt. With right sides together, join the binding strips as shown below.

Joining binding strips

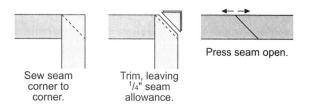

Sew seam corner to corner. Trim, leaving $^{1}/_{4}$" seam allowance. Press seam open.

Fold the binding in half lengthwise with wrong sides together and press, taking care not to stretch the fabric. At one end, open out the fold and turn the raw edge in at a 45° angle. Press. Trim, leaving a $^{1}/_{4}$" seam allowance.

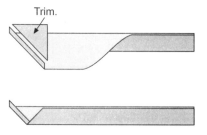
Trim.

Beginning on one edge of the quilt a few inches from a corner, pin the binding to the quilt top. Beginning two inches from the folded end of the binding, stitch $^{3}/_{8}$" from the raw edges and stop $^{3}/_{8}$" from the raw edge at the corner. Backstitch and remove the quilt.

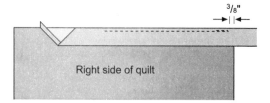
$^{3}/_{8}$"

Right side of quilt

Fold the binding back on itself to create a 45° angle, then turn the binding down to make a fold in the binding that is in line with the upper raw edge of the quilt top. Pin. Stitch the binding to the quilt, ending $^{3}/_{8}$" from the next corner. Backstitch and miter the corner as you did the previous one.

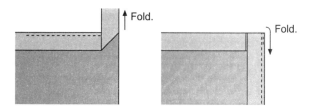
Fold. Fold.

Continue in this manner until the binding has been stitched to all four edges of the quilt top. When you reach the beginning of the binding, trim away excess, leaving 1" to tuck into the folded binding. Complete the stitching.

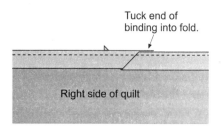
Tuck end of binding into fold.

Right side of quilt

Turn the binding to the back of the quilt. Hand sew in place, using a blind stitch, and mitering corners as shown.

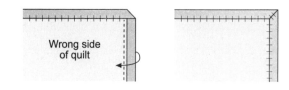
Wrong side of quilt